3-D THRILLERS!

BIG CATS
and Amazing Jungle Animals

SAMANTHA HILTON

■ SCHOLASTIC

New York • Toronto • London • Auckland
Sydney • Mexico City • New Delhi • Hong Kong

SO WHAT IS

Cats are meat-eating hunters with sharp claws and agile bodies. The cat family includes 37 different species, and at the top of the feline pile are the big cats—tigers, lions, cheetahs, leopards, cougars, and jaguars.

▼ Fancy a dip?

In addition to big prey such as buffalo, tigers also like to catch fish. Some cats hate the water, but on a hot, steamy day, there's nothing a tiger likes better than cooling off!

A BIG CAT?

Vanishing act ▶

Spotty or stripy, or even a plain dusty brown color, a cat's coat has one main purpose—to help it hide from its prey. A leopard's spotted coat is excellent camouflage. Leopards will often lie in a tree until an unsuspecting animal, such as a wild pig or antelope, passes below. Then the leopard drops silently down onto its prey, moving in for the kill.

◀ Motherly love

A lioness takes good care of her young and keeps them hidden in a den for the first six weeks of their lives. Like kittens, lion cubs are born blind and helpless, which makes them vulnerable to attacks from predators such as hyenas, jackals, and even eagles.

TIGERS—BIG

The tiger is the biggest of all the big cats and is easily the most recognizable, with its orange, black, and white stripy body. There are five species of tiger, but the Siberian, or Amur, tiger is the biggest. It can grow up to 13 feet (4 m) long and weigh as much as four people!

Purrr-fect parent ▶

Like most big cats, tigers prefer to be alone—except when a tigress is raising her young. A tiger cub stays with its mother for around two years, until it's old enough to leave her to find its own territory. During those years, the mother teaches her cub essential survival skills, including how to stalk and hunt prey.

CAT GIANTS

Male tigers mark their TERRITORY by scraping deep marks on trees with their sharp claws, sending a clear warning to all rivals!

Watch the whiskers ▶

A tiger's whiskers can tell you what kind of mood the animal is in. If it's relaxed, they turn down and at right angles to the tiger's face. If the tiger is hunting, its whiskers stand straight up and spread out!

KING OF THE

The lion is often called the king of the jungle, and with its regal appearance it's easy to see why. Lions may not be the biggest cats, but they are kings of their own territories. They used to be more widespread, but now lions are found mainly in Africa and one area of India.

▼ One big family

Lions are much more sociable than tigers and are the only big cats to live in family groups. These are called prides, and at the head of each pride is a dominant male lion. Each pride has several lionesses, who hunt and take care of the cubs.

JUNGLE

▼ Mane attraction

Male lions are the only big cats with manes, and scientists are still trying to figure out what they're for! A mane may help protect a lion's neck in fights with other males.

Lion cubs are born with faint brown spots, called ROSETTES, on their coats. They fade away as the cubs grow.

THE SOLITARY

Leopards are the most adaptable of the big cats and are found in all sorts of places—jungles, grasslands, and even icy mountaintops. Leopards are solitary hunters, stalking anything from lizards to baby giraffes.

▼ Black magic

Some leopards are born almost black in color and are called panthers. No one knows why, but more panthers are born in areas with thick jungles. Perhaps a dark coat is harder to see there? If you looked closely at a panther's coat (not recommended in the wild!), you would see that it still has rosettes.

HUNTER

▲ Ice-loving cat

There are more than 20 species of leopard, and they come in all shapes and sizes, depending on where they live. The snow leopard lives high in the mountains of central Asia, including the Himalayas. It has powerful legs and is able to leap 50 feet (15 m) to catch its prey! Its body is insulated by thick hair, and its wide, fur-covered feet act as natural snowshoes.

Treetop pantry ▶

After making a kill, a leopard will drag its catch up into a tree, safe from the reach of a lion on the lookout for a free lunch. It takes enormous strength, as a kill can sometimes weigh up to three times as much as the leopard itself!

LEAN, SPEEDY

T he cheetah is a sleek, lightning-fast hunting machine. Once, cheetahs were found sprinting all over Africa, the Middle East, and India. But poaching and the loss of their homes to farming mean these champion runners have become an endangered species.

▼ Record-breaking cat

Cheetahs are the world's fastest land animals and can reach speeds of around 62 miles (100 km) per hour—that's nearly as fast as cars can legally travel on a freeway! This is handy for chasing prey, but a cheetah can't run this fast for long and usually gives up after about 20 seconds.

Unlike their lion cousins, cheetahs cannot ROAR. Instead, they purr, hiss, whine, and growl.

MACHINE

◄ Paws off!

Once a cheetah has made a kill, it needs to eat quickly and keep an eye out for scavengers. Given half a chance, lions, leopards, hyenas, baboons, and jackals won't hesitate to rob a cheetah of its lunch. With its weak jaws and small teeth, a cheetah can't fight off larger predators.

Hunting lessons ►

Most big cat mothers teach their young the skills they need to survive in the wild. But a mother cheetah really wants her cubs to become successful hunters. She will even catch and keep prey alive for her cubs to use as hunting practice!

AMERICA'S BIG

The athletic cougar is the most widespread of American big cats. You'll find cougars prowling all the way from southern Canada to Patagonia at the bottom of South America. Cougars are also known as mountain lions, pumas, and panthers.

▲ Meaty meal

Cougars are not fussy eaters and will eat almost anything, from deer and beavers to insects and even snails. Cougars can eat up to 10 pounds (4.5 kg) of meat in one day. That's about 40 hamburgers!

◀ Buried treasure

Once a cougar has made a kill, it doesn't want to lose it to another predator. So it buries its food under a big pile of leaves and dirt. With its dinner safely hidden, the cougar can return to it each night until every last bite has been devoured.

12

KITTY CAT

Pain in the neck ▶

Cougars like to sneak up on their prey in the same way other big cats do. When its prey is close by, the cougar pounces with one mighty leap. But unlike other big cats, a cougar does not strangle its prey—it breaks its neck with one bite from its powerful jaws!

NIGHTTIME

T he jaguar is one of South America's fiercest predators. This deadly night hunter lives mainly in dark jungle areas where it uses its excellent vision to track down its food. Like most big cats, the jaguar hunts alone, usually on the ground, but it leaps into the trees if it needs to.

▼ Headache!

Most cats, including jaguars, kill by biting their prey around the throat, tightening their jaws, and suffocating them. But the jaguar has another, unique way of killing—it closes its teeth around its prey's head and pierces its brain. Ouch!

PROWLER

Gone fishing ▶

Jaguars will eat most animals, from mice and deer to frogs and alligators. They have also developed a clever method of fishing. The jaguar waits by the water and waves its tail over the surface. The motion attracts fish, which the jaguar then scoops out of the water with its claws.

◀ Spot the difference

Jaguars are often confused with leopards, but not only do they live on different continents, jaguars are much heavier cats. There is also a slight difference in their spotty coats. Both jaguars and leopards have a rosette pattern, but it is the inside of the rosettes that gives the game away—jaguars have smaller spots within the rosettes, and leopards don't.

WHHT IS THE

J aguars and some leopards live in dense jungles, which are also known as tropical rain forests. There are rain forests in Africa, Central and South America, Asia, and Australia.

▼ World's jungles

Jungles, or tropical rain forests, are found only in a narrow band on either side of the equator—an imaginary line that goes around the middle of the earth.

Central America
Africa
Southeast Asia
South America
Equator
Australia

◀ A living jungle

Rain forests, as the name suggests, are very wet places, and all this water brings with it an amazing variety of plant and animal life. Rain forests cover only about 6 percent of the earth's surface, but they contain more than 50 percent of all forms of life on the planet, from insects to big cats, reptiles to toucans!

JUNGLE?

Layers and ... ▶

A rain forest is split into levels, like a four-story building. At the bottom is the forest floor, where giant anteaters live. The next layer, the understory, is home to small plants and trees and millions of insects, which make it very noisy!

... layers ▶

Then comes the canopy, which contains tall trees and is bursting with life, such as colorful toucans and chattering monkeys. Finally, the emergent layer is home to the tallest trees, some of which grow over 200 feet (70 m) high!

THE AMAZING

T he Amazon rain forest in South America is the biggest in the world. Together with the Central American rain forest, these two areas have the largest range of amazing animals found on the earth.

The AMAZON RIVER, which flows through the rain forest, is home to thousands of animals, including river dolphins, turtles, and ferocious PIRANHA FISH.

▼ Eagle-eyed predator

The fearsome harpy eagle is one of the world's largest eagles, and it lives in the treetops of Central and South America. This eagle has hind talons that can be the size of grizzly bear claws. It is so powerful it can catch howler monkeys and sloths and feed them to its young!

AMAZON

▲ Toxic frog

There are more than 170 species of poison dart frog. The bright colors of the deadly strawberry poison dart frog, which lives in Central America, warn predators not to eat it.

Noisy neighbors ▶

Howler monkeys are the noisiest animals in the rain forest. They begin calling at dawn or dusk and can be heard up to 3 miles (5 km) away!

DEEP DOWN IN

Most of the African rain forest is found near the Congo River in central Africa. As the world's second largest rain forest, it's home to some incredible animals, including gorillas, parrots, and deadly snakes!

▶ Gentle giant

Gorillas are the largest of all the apes, and they live in family groups called troops in the forests of central Africa. The troop is led by a large, dominant male, called a silverback due to the silver-gray hairs on his back. Gorillas are peaceful animals that spend most of their day looking for young plants and juicy shoots to eat.

THE JUNGLE

Chatty parrot ▶

The gray parrot is one of the most talkative and talented parrots on earth. Not only can it repeat human words perfectly, it can also mimic the sounds made by electronic devices such as telephones and alarm clocks! Unfortunately, this ability has made it a very popular pet, and it is fast becoming one of the African rain forest's many endangered animals.

◀ Fangsss!

This African tree snake can shoot venom through large fangs that are found in the rear of its jaw. The snake sleeps during the day and hunts at night, feeding on lizards, bats, frogs, and small mammals. Luckily, it is not really dangerous to humans!

THE JUNGLES

The rain forests of Asia stretch from India to Indonesia and down to New Guinea. These vast jungles are noisy with the calls of orangutans, monkeys, frogs, birds, and tiny insects.

▼ Jungle swinger

The orangutan is often called the old man of the forest. This shy ape rarely comes down to the ground. Instead, it is happiest swinging through the trees—and with arms that reach 7 feet (2 m) from fingertip to fingertip, it is definitely suited to a life in the tall trees of Southeast Asia!

◀ Leaf mimic

Leaf insects are about 4 inches (10 cm) long and have flat, irregularly shaped bodies, with markings that make them look like leaves. They feed on plants and can even sway in the wind like real leaves.

Spot the predator ▶

Many jungle animals use camouflage to hide in the shadows—this is as true of big predators as it is of insects. The clouded leopard's bold markings may stand out in a safari park, but in its natural home those spots match the light and shade of the jungle perfectly.

HUSTRALIA'S

Australia's rain forest may be small compared to others found across the world, but it's just as spectacular. Australia is home to many unusual animals, and some, such as the kangaroo, are found only in this part of the world.

▲ Night crawler

The ringtail possum is unique to the Australian rain forest. At night, it creeps through the forest in search of food, using its long, curled tail to help it climb and jump across the branches. During the day, the possum curls up in a tight ball and sleeps on a branch.

◄ Hopping along

The last place you would expect to see a kangaroo is in a tree, but that is exactly where you'll find them in this rain forest. There are two species of tree kangaroo in Australia, and some are so well adapted to life in the branches that they can barely hop on the ground anymore!

LOST WORLD

The **AUSTRALIAN JUNGLE** is home to the largest reptile on earth—the **SALTWATER CROCODILE**. It can grow to 23 feet (7 m) in length!

▲ Feeling blue

Rain forests are home to many insects, and some of the most colorful are the butterflies. One of the stars of the Australian jungle is the Ulysses butterfly, or the mountain blue as it is known. Being such a vivid blue color—and measuring almost 6 inches (15 cm) across—it's one of the easier animals to spot in the rain forest.

LIVING IN THE

R ain forests are home to more than just amazing plants and animals. Around 50 million people also call the jungle their home. Grouped into around 1,000 different tribes, these people have had to learn how to live in a difficult environment.

▼ Forest homes

If you know what to look for, the rain forest can provide all the food, medicine, clothing, and building materials you need to survive. This house in Papua New Guinea is built from branches, rushes, and other materials found in the rain forest.

JUNGLE

Living together ▶

In some rain forests, old enemies are learning to live together. Big cats, such as tigers, can be important to the local economy because they attract tourism. So, instead of killing tigers for their skins, local people work hard to preserve the tiger's natural environment.

Five hundred years ago, there were about 10 million NATIVE PEOPLE living in the Amazon rain forest. Today there are less than 200,000!

Protect our homes ▶

Industry and logging have destroyed large areas of rain forest. Now, some Amazon rain forest tribes are fighting back. Their protests have secured the protection of part of the forests for their people.

JUNGLES IN

R ain forests across the world are shrinking rapidly, and it is all due to humans. It is possible that rain forests and the animals that live there will be wiped out within 50 years—and then we will all be in deep trouble!

▼ Timber!

The greatest threat to rain forests comes from logging. Huge areas of South America's rain forest—larger than some countries—have been cut down to supply timber or to create farmland. Rain forest soil is not very fertile, so once the land is exhausted, even more forest has to be cleared to grow new crops.

There are some ENVIRONMENTALISTS who estimate that an area the size of a FOOTBALL FIELD is cleared in the rain forest every second!

DANGER

◄ Under threat

In the Asian rain forests, many big cats are threatened with extinction. Some are hunted for their skins, to make clothes or rugs, or for their bones and teeth, which are used in some traditional medicines. Even though big cats are protected by law, they are still hunted by poachers.

Homeless ►

In the rain forests of Africa, many animals, such as this baby gorilla, are losing their territory as the human population grows. People cut down the forest to create more farmland, and they can also carry diseases that they pass on to the gorillas.

FUN FACTS!

Now that you've prowled with the big cats and explored the rain forests, you probably think you know it all. Well, here are even more incredible facts!

Pepper, oranges, chocolate, pineapples, cucumbers, coffee, and even chewing gum all came from RAIN FORESTS!

▲ Masters of disguise

Chameleons are amazing jungle lizards that can change the color of their skin depending on their mood or the temperature! These forest-dwelling reptiles can flash pink, blue, red, orange, green, and even black!